DRESS YOU UP

30 simple accessories to make and wear

rosy nicholas

Photography by Adam Laycock

quadrille

CONTENTS

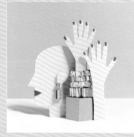

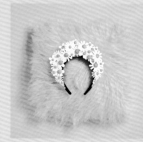

INTRODUCTION

This is me, age 8, at my popstars-themed birthday party, dressed up as my favourite female star of the time, Madonna. Wearing an extraordinary amount of make up, a can of white hairspray, a pair of yellow converse chucks… and this Jean Paul Gaultier knock off, hand sewn by my mother.

For me, dressing up has always been associated with having a good time, from age 8 to now. I still like to draw on my eyebrows and make myself things to wear.

I've always been interested in costume and traditional dress. It's the cabinet in any museum where you can truly see how crackers human beings are. The time and detail we put into making elaborate and ornate things to wear goes back centuries. Historically and culturally, it signals something special is happening: a ceremony, a celebration, a performance.

I am a child of the music video generation and grew up in the age of the glamorous superstar. My idols were Michael and Janet Jackson, Prince, and Madonna; all the heavyweights of their time, whose outfits were as important to them as their music. During my youth, I spent hours watching television, blockbuster movies and VHS tapes of concerts. The 80s and 90s were full of excess; big popstars who wore big outfits — no doubt, the inspiration for the MORE IS MORE philosophy I still stand by today!

I was lucky to have parents who encouraged and facilitated all my early making. Dad – born into the glamour of 60s Iran – kept a front room full of vinyl and art books, the walls of the house covered in patterned wallpaper and prints, and the floors in bright Persian carpets. He was our pop culture educator, always encouraging us to stay up late to watch telly and recording countless movies for us on tape. My first trip to the Harrods Egyptian room and seeing Michael

Jackson at Wembley are my earliest visual memories. Dad was all about seeing new things and having a groovy time.

Mum was just good at everything; a girl who grew up in a family full of women, who were all excellent at crafts and making beautiful things by hand. Sewing, knitting, cooking, baking, drawing – you wanted something, she could make it better than the shops. We had a dressing-up box bursting with handmade costumes and dinners arranged on the plate into a smiley face. The birthday cakes were so good that other mums started paying her to make them for their kids. Creative and nurturing, she is easily the best teacher I've ever had.

Our house was full of art materials, and if I was bored I was told to make something. Craft was always my favourite form of play, and, lucky for me, I've somehow managed to turn it into my job.

Now, as an adult, making things that I also get to wear is such a bonus. The enjoyment I get from the making process is equal to that of how I feel wearing it.

My choice of materials has also changed very little with time. I still choose inexpensive things from the art shop that I can turn from the everyday into a fun and special piece that no one else in the world has. It may mean that some of the accessories won't last forever, but nothing good does. I hope that you party them to pieces and then just make more!

I'm sure my parents look back at this photo of me and wonder (as we all are) what the hell they were thinking!

But it's thanks to these two, and the generation I was born into, that I grew up with a taste for the opulent, and the tools to recreate it for myself. I think they understood that I was just doing what Madonna told me to, and I hope this book helps you to do the same – have fun and EXPRESS YOURSELF!

To mum and dad, thank you for falling in love at art school and letting me watch MTV.

Dress You Up -
one of my favourite
Madonna songs, and
a perfect title for
this book!

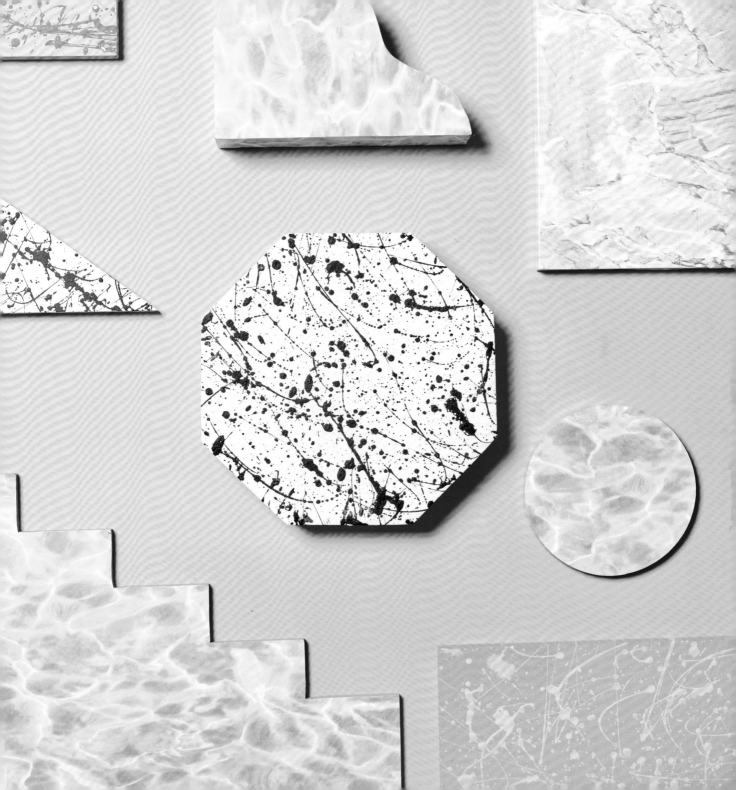

TOP SHOPPING TIPS

Shopping for materials is one of my favourite things about being a maker. I probably spend most of my time in art and craft shops but I'm lucky to live in London, which has an amazing selection of wonderful haberdashers and markets to get excited in. I've always loved shopping, specifically anywhere I can rummage alone for hours through boxes of weird old stuff, so I love charity shops and pound shops too. Making glitzy things to wear with inexpensive materials is my favourite kind of project, so here are some top tips on my favourite materials and the more unusual places to shop your way to opulence on a budget.

Alice bands (1) They're a bit trickier to find, but I'm staying loyal to these 80s-style velvet-covered padded alice bands. Hairbands covered in any fabric hold onto the glue so much better than plastic ones, so I'd recommend getting them if you can; you can pretty much stick anything to one of these. I find them in chemists, hair and beauty shops and quite easily online.

Clasps (2) Putting clasps on your accessories isn't essential, but I think it finishes things off nicely; my preferred taste is the bigger the better. Most haberdashers and craft shops will stock findings and clasps, but I like to shop around in less likely places such as theatrical chandlers, fitting and DIY shops. A big heavy clasp can make your piece look so much more expensive and professional — especially good for impressing pals when making them a gift.

DIY shops (3) Don't ask me why DIY shops are one of the best places to find pastel-coloured, scented bin bags, but it is a fact! They're a good source of lots of other surprisingly useful things too, like really cheap reels of coloured cord and chain and patterned vinyls, as well as a great range of strong glues, spray paints and varnishes.

Haberdasheries and markets (4) Street markets always seem to be best for bright colours and glitzy finds such as fur and marabou. As with the wool, I find the cheaper places often have a much more fun selection, so I think they're great places for crafters. A trip to the haberdashery on the market is always a treat for a magpie like me, and it's so important to keep our local ones alive, so, please go rummage and support your local trimming shops and markets.

Homeware shops (5) Homeware shops often stock items designed for decorating the home, that are great for craft projects. I always keep a vase of fake flowers in my studio; they are affordable, look pretty and last forever. As they're fabric, they will stick to almost anything with the aid of a glue gun. The flowers I've used for my crown are from Hobbycraft, who have a great selection, but you can also find them in lots of homeware shops, and pound shops.

Model shops (6) Model shops are a great source of weird materials that you won't find anywhere else. They're a much more technical and precise sort of place than an art shop, but they always have interesting plastics, rolls of weird films and different polystyrene shapes, not to mention packs of miniature trees! Gotta make something with them...

Party shops (7) My local party shop is one of my favourite places in the world! Everything is bright, fun, shiny, over the top and made for celebration. These sheets of foil are probably meant for wrapping presents, but I use them all the time for accessories. Most of the decorations they stock, I'd essentially just like to put straight on my head!

Supermarkets (8) Even a trip to the supermarket can result in finding great craft materials. I use straws alot; I love them because they're cheap, hardy and come in great colours. If you haven't got a party shop near you, supermarkets often have a good party section, with brightly coloured straws and other sorts of fun table wear.

Wool (9) If you're already a knitter, then these crafts are perfect for using up odds and ends of wool. I only ever really buy wool for craft purposes, so I always want them in bright colours and don't tend to worry too much about quality. In fact, for some reason, in my experience the cheaper the wool, the better the colours! So, don't feel like you need to get expensive stuff. I usually buy good old affordable DK wool.

MASTER MAKES

In this section you will find my favourite simple crafts. They are incredibly useful to learn, as each one can be used as a quick stand-alone project or combined with other elements to make a more complicated piece, such as the accessories that appear in this book.

These projects are really versatile; you can achieve a whole range of effects, depending on the size you go for and the materials you choose. They are all fun and inexpensive to make, and deeply satisfying – I use them all the time. If you can get to grips with these essentials, before you know it you'll be a craft master!

How to make a tassel

1. Cut a piece of card the length that you want your tassel.

2. Wrap some wool around the length of the card, about 20 times — the more you wrap, the thicker your tassel will be.

3. When you've got to the desired amount, cut the thread.

4. Weave another length of wool between the wound thread and the card.

5. Then tie in a knot at the top.

6. Cut the lengths of thread along the other end of the card, then remove from the card.

7. Tie another piece of thread around the top of the strands, to gather them together, and tie in a knot.

8. Bring the ends down to blend in with the tassel and trim.

Tassel making is quick, easy and addictive, and you can use all kinds of wools and threads. Come and join me in a world where everything is better with a tassel on it!

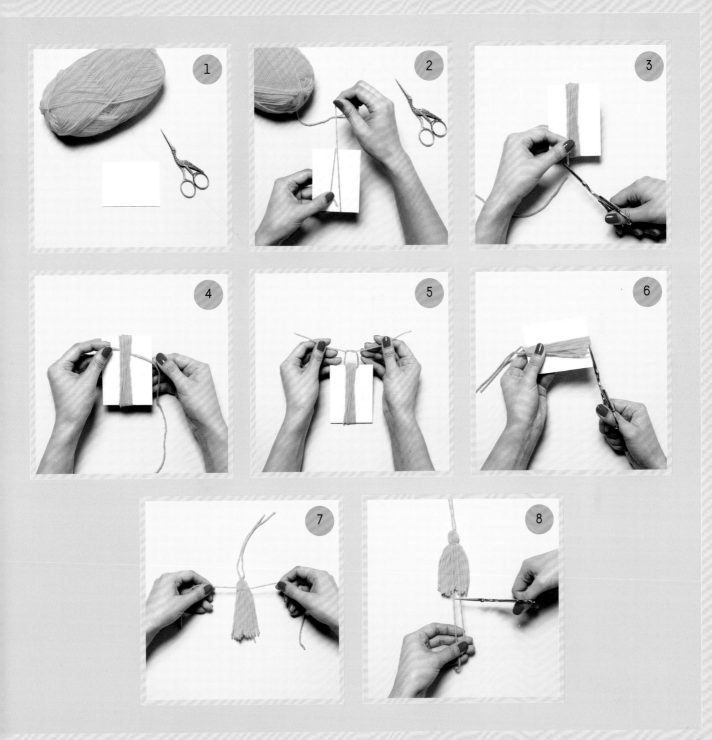

How to make a wool pompom

Sometimes I long for days gone by, when it took me an extraordinary amount of time to make just one pompom. Perhaps its nostalgia, or that weird enjoyable pain that people like us get from making something that takes hours. Either way, the need for two rings of cardboard and the length of the entire summer holidays to make a few pompoms are a thing of the past... because now we have the pompom maker! This is the perfect gadget for a long journey, or watching TV, and it will have you popping these guys out like nobody's business.

Thread them into a necklace

Glue gun to a hairband

Try these simple pompom accessory ideas

1. Open up one half of the pompom maker fully.

2. Take one end of your wool and, starting at one end, wrap the wool evenly round the crescent shape until you get to the other end.

3. Keep working back and forth to fill the pompom maker, until it's nice and plump like a satsuma segment. Cut the thread.

4. Close up this side, then open up the other side and repeat.

5. Use scissors to cut the threads all the way round the maker.

6. Cut another length of wool, slip it between the two halves of the pompom maker and tie it round the middle, pulling tight to make sure the knot sinks into the centre of the maker.

7. Tie another knot to secure. Open up the arms of the pompom maker and pull apart in the middle. Your pompom should pop out.

8. Trim any long ends so you have a perfect sphere.

9. Get POMPOM-ING!

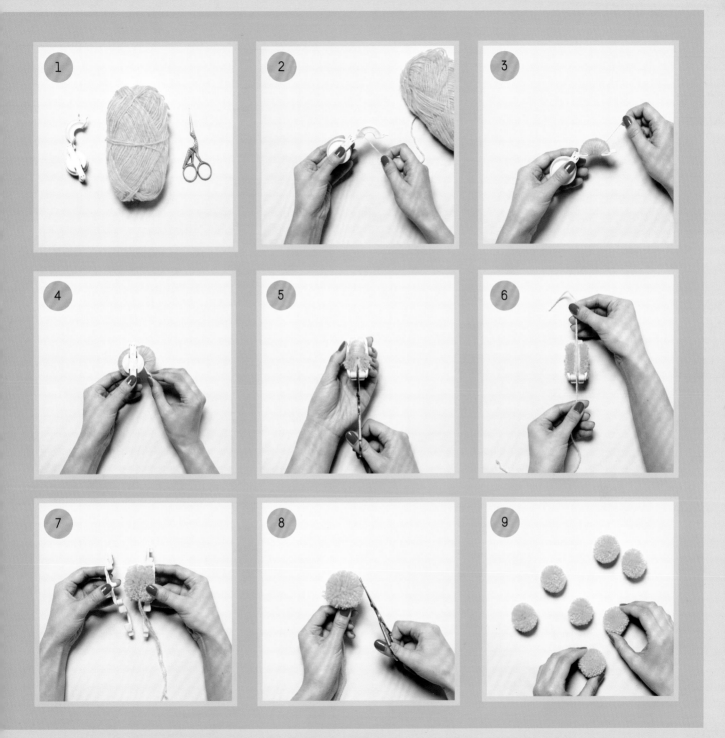

How to make a paper pompom

These can be used for so many things: gift wrapping, party decorations and, of course, accessories!

The great thing about these paper pompoms is that you don't need exact measurements – I suggest simply folding your tissue paper in half continuously until you have roughly the right size for your project. You can tell what sort of size your pompom will be by the width of your sheets of tissue.

This works really well with tissue paper, but you can also use any thin acetate, foil or film.

1. Fold some tissue paper in half, then repeat until it is about A5 (or whatever size you need for your project) and cut along all the folded edges so you have loose sheets.

2. Place 10 layers in a neat stack, then fold every 2cm (¾in) in alternate directions, to form a concertina.

3. Wind a piece of wire round the centre of the concertina, then twist the ends to secure.

4. Round off the ends of the paper using scissors.

5. Fan open the concertina on both sides.

6. Holding the wire, carefully lift up one tissue layer at a time, on one side and then repeat on the other side.

7. Depending on your project, leave your pom on the wire to attach it to things otherwise trim the wire ends, if you want to stick them flat. Pull the pompom through your hands and use the wire as a stem, to create a flower.

PROJECTS

FLOWER CROWNS

These flower crowns look a lot more complicated than they actually are.

If you spend a bit of time collecting a nice bunch, along with some little extra bits, then it's hard to mess it up. I always start by getting my large flowers in colours that compliment each other, then search for the smaller pieces in weird places. All the berries and tiny flowers shown here, were found at my local cake decorating shop.

As you're making your hairband, keep trying it on and having a look in the mirror; it will help you to get a nice shape and balance that works from all angles.

Things you need

selection of fake flowers
   (around 5 large flowers and
   then a mix of smaller ones)
pliers
alice band
glue gun

1. Collect all your flowers together and trim the stems, using pilers, to a manageable length — about 3cm [1⅛in].

2. Lay your alice band flat and arrange the flowers around it until you are happy with your composition. Place the largest flowers at the top and the smaller flowers down the sides of the band.

3. Take your centre flower and using a glue gun, glue an area of about 2cm [¾in] square. Then place the flower onto the glue at a slight diagonal, pressing for about 15 seconds until the glue cools off.

4. Now continue by gluing on your next largest flowers, nestling them next to the centre flower, and working like this all the way down the side of the band.

5. For extra security, add small blobs of glue under some of the petals and in-between flowers so everything is well attached.

6. Look at the hairband from all angles; you may want to add a few smaller flowers that face directly out to the sides, to fill any holes or hide any unsightly patches.

7. Use some of the leaves from your flowers to cover any stems or gluey bits that are visible from the back.

TA-DAH!

Try using only one type of flower like this rose one.

POM
STRAW
DISC MIX

This is a trio of elements that look great together, in any order, so you can make up your own combinations and colourways.

I've given you a few examples, but mix it up and make a lot; they look really good layered up together.

Things you need

wool, in any colours
  of your choice
pompom maker
coloured drinking straws
scissors
large needle
small coin, 2.5cm
  [1in] in diameter
coloured card
pencil
compass cutter (optional)

1. Make seven pompoms, using the instructions provided on page 14. Cut the drinking straws into 4cm [1½in] lengths.

2. In a different colour wool, make three tassels, following the instructions on page 12. Thread your needle, then push it through a pompom and then a straw. Repeat until you have seven pompoms and six straws on your wool.

3. Thread one of the tassels ends onto your needle, and push the needle up through your middle pompom.

4. Tie a knot in the tassel ends and trim them enough so they are hidden within your pompom.

5. Attach the two remaining tassels, one on each end. Tie a knot around the main thread and trim the ends, or thread them back into the neighbouring pompom.

6. Place the coin on the card and draw round it 26 times, then cut out the circles with scissors. Alternatively, use a compass cutter set to 3.5cm [1⅜in].

7. Cut the drinking straws at 2cm [¾in] lengths and thread alternatively with the discs. Add a tassel or a pompom to the centre or ends, if you wish.

These are addictive to make — the more the merrier!

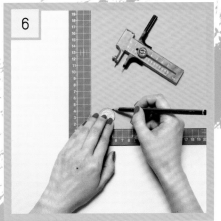

CHRISTMAS PARTY POMS

December – so many people, so many parties!

A girl needs to be ready with some instant festive glamour at all times, and this is my last-minute Christmas classic. Christmas is also one of the best times to go shopping for materials. There is an abundance of glitzy, glittery and cheap decorations in the shops, which are perfect for a quick accessory make. Pound shops are probably my favourite place this season, and they always have good tinsel.

Things you need

needle and thread
tinsel, 20cm [8in] per pompom
black elastic or cable ties
1 pair of shoes
scissors
glue gun
hairband

1. Cut 20cm [8in] of tinsel. Thread your needle with a double length of thread, and sew a few stitches into one end of the tinsel so the thread is secure, creating a solid anchor.

2. Push the spine of the tinsel onto the needle, close to your starting point, and pull the thread through.

3. Now, using this image as an example, concertina the tinsel onto your needle by pushing through the tinsels central spine.

4. Pull the thread through the tinsel and repeat step 3 again, until you get to the end of your tinsel.

5. Push the concertinaed tinsel down to your starting end so that it all bunches up into a ball shape. Hold in this position and put in a few stitches to hold it all together, then knot.

6. Take your elastic or cable tie and thread it through the tinsel pom from one side to the other.

7. Attach the poms by fastening the cable tie to the front strap of your shoe or tie it on with the elastic. Trim the ends and repeat steps 1-6 for your other shoe.

8. For the hairband, make two more poms. Add a large circle of glue onto your hairband, in the position you want to attach your poms. Push the tinsel pom onto the glue and hold in place until the glue has set.

Add to any outfit and you're Christmas party ready!

DECO BANGLES AND EARRINGS

I love making things out of mirrored card; it folds and scores really well, so it's perfect for constructing shapes – and, who doesn't love a metallic finish? I wanted to make Art Deco-style jewellery, and I think the silver works really well here, but you could use any kind of card.

A compass cutter is an excellent investment for this project. It's not essential, but is so much quicker than drawing and cutting out discs and gives perfect results. I use discs of card throughout this book, so investing in this handy tool is definitely my top gadget tip.

Things you need: Bracelets

A3 sheet of mirri card
small coin, about 2.5cm
  [1in] in diameter
scissors or a compass cutter
ruler
scalpel
very strong double-sided tape
paper clip
pencil

Things you need: Earrings

A3 sheet of mirri card
pencil
ruler
scissors or a compass cutter
scalpel
very strong double-sided tape
4 headpins
pliers
small coin, about 2.5cm
  [1in] in diameter
glue gun and superglue
2 earring fittings

1. Draw round a small coin, about 2.5cm [1in] in diameter, 54 times on the back of your mirri card. Cut out with scissors or use a compass cutter, to cut out each disc.

2. Score a straight line down the middle of each disc, on the shiny side, using a ruler and scalpel. If you've used a compass cutter your centre point will be marked already.

3. Gently fold the discs down along the scored line.

4. Take two discs and stick them plain side together on one half of your fold, using a good amount of double-sided tape.

5. Attach another disc in the same way, and continue until you have six discs attached to form an open semi-sphere. Repeat with the remaining discs until you have nine semi-spheres.

6. Cut a strip of mirri card 26 x 2.5cm [10$\frac{1}{4}$ x 1in]. Fit the strip around your wrist, inside out so the ends overlap. Adjust so it slips on and off easily. Hold in place with a paper clip and mark the end with a pencil.

7. Now work out your spacing by placing your spheres along the strip, until you hit the pencil mark. I used all nine spheres and overlapped their edges slightly. Everyone will differ, depending on their wrist-size.

8. Stick the ends of your strip together with more tape. Then stick the flat sides of the first semi-sphere to your bracelet. Continue to work round the bracelet adding the semi-spheres as you go.

Experiment with different-sized discs or how many you use for each semi-sphere, or even what shape you cut - squares work well, too!

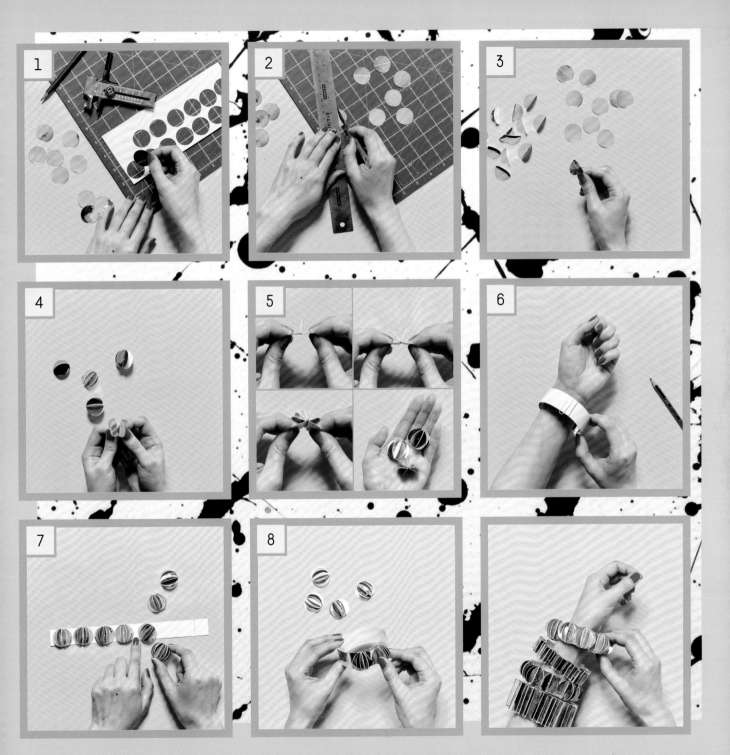

1. On the reverse of your mirri card, draw 20 rectangles measuring 4 x 3cm [1½ x 1⅛in]. Cut them out using a scalpel or scissors. Then use a scalpel and ruler, score each rectangle down the middle. Fold all along the scored line.

2. Take two rectangles and stick the white sides together with tape on one half. Attach another rectangle. Continue until you have 10 rectangles attached on all sides to form a complete column. Repeat to make another column.

3. Cut two more small discs from the card 1cm [⅜in] in diameter. Take two headpins and thread one small disc onto each one, then thread the pin through each column.

4. Use pliers to bend the tops of the headpins to form hooks at the top of the column.

5. On the reverse of your mirri paper, use a pencil and draw round the small coin 14 times, then cut out your discs using scissors. Or use a compass cutter with a diameter of 2.5cm [1in].

6. Using 12 of your discs, follow steps 2-5 on page 34, make two open semi-spheres of six discs.

7. Bend a headpin in half, creating a U-shape and trim the ends. Tape this onto one of your remaining discs then cover this whole area with glue and stick on one of your spheres.

8. Connect the loop at the base of the sphere to the hook at the top of the column, and close the hook with pliers to secure. Use superglue at attach an earring fitting to the back of the disc near the top edge.

9. Repeat steps 7 and 8 for the second earring.

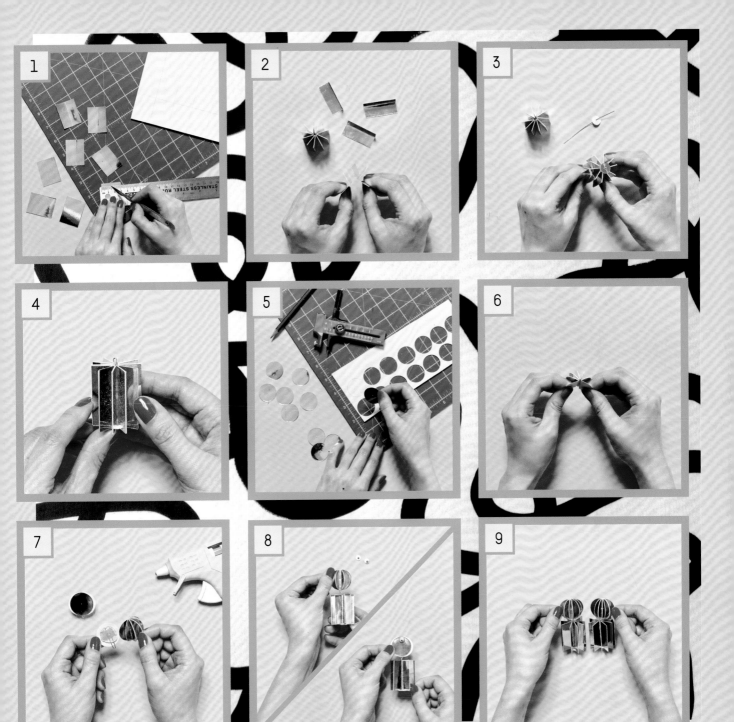

GLITTER BALL EARRINGS & RING

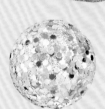

Glitter is probably the love of my life!

My first proper job after college was at a props house, where I had to glitter massive polystyrene shapes for parties, an absolute dream! I've been hooked on the stuff ever since and I think most things in life look better glittered.

The mount board shape you cut can be anything you like. I've done a pair of red sparkly lips for a hint of 80s glamour.

Things you need

3 polystyrene balls
skewer or bradawl
paint, in a similar colour to your glitter
PVA glue and superglue
paintbrush
glitter
2 sequins
4 headpins
pilers
small piece of mount board or heavy card
wire cutters
double-sided tape
glue gun
2 earring fittings
2 jump rings
1 ring finding

1. To make the first earring, take one polystyrene ball and, using a skewer, make a hole all the way through the middle. Keep the ball on the skewer to make it easier to paint.

2. Mix a little paint into your glue, to give it a solid base. Paint the ball with the glue and while still wet, sprinkle glitter all over so it's well coated. Stand the ball in a glass, to dry. Repeat steps 1-2 for the other ball.

3. When both balls are dry, remove the skewers. Thread a sequin onto each headpin, then push the pins through the hole in the ball. Bend the top of the headpin over, using pilers to make a loop.

4. Take the mount board and cut out four identical shapes like these lips, see page 123 for the template.

5. Take a headpin and using wire cutters, trim and bend to make an S-shape with loops at the top and bottom of the wire. Attach the jump ring and the earring fitting to the top loop. Use tape, to stick it to your lips, as shown.

6. Using the glue gun, stick another lip shape on top of the headpin, sandwiching it between the two pieces of board. Repeat steps 5-6 for the second earring. Following step 2, paint both of your shapes with glue and glitter. Leave to dry.

7. For the ring, stick the smaller polystyrene ball to a cocktail stick, paint with the glue mixture as in step 2 and add glitter. Stand the ball in a glass, to dry.

8. When dry, remove from the stick and superglue to a ring finding.

9. To finish the earrings hook the glitter ball and the glitter lips together, and close the loops with pilers to secure.

DAISY QUEEN

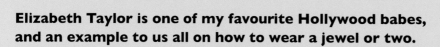

Elizabeth Taylor is one of my favourite Hollywood babes, and an example to us all on how to wear a jewel or two.

This hairband was heavily influenced by a photo I found of her, wearing a most fabulous Bulgari headpiece, covered in tiny jewelled daisies, that blew my mind. Liz owned one of the most incredible jewellery collections ever, so I figured if it was good enough for Liz... I made this slightly more modest version for myself to wear at my Egyptian-themed birthday party – I felt just like Cleopatra.

Things you need

2 sheets of A4 white card
templates from pages 123 and 125
pencil
scissors
25 small polystyrene or pulp balls
scalpel
glue gun
yellow or gold paint
PVA glue
paintbrush
gold glitter
A4 white felt
toy stuffing
needle and white thread
alice band

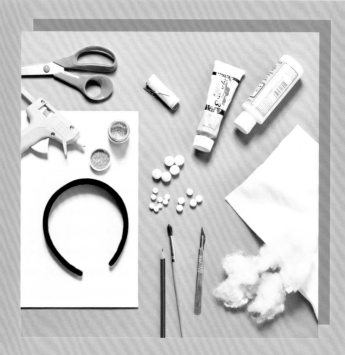

1. Using the daisy templates provided on page 123, draw about 50 daisies in various sizes on the card, then cut them out using scissors.

2. Cut your polystyrene balls in half using a scalpel, and stick them to your daisy centres using a glue gun. Alternatively, you could make your centres using fimo or something similar.

3. Mix a pea-sized amount of yellow or gold paint into some PVA glue, and paint it onto the centre of your daisies with a paintbrush. Work in small batches of about five at a time.

4. While the glue is still wet, sprinkle glitter over the top, making sure the daisy centres are well covered, then shake it off. Repeat this process for the remaining daisies. Leave them all to dry.

5. Using the templates on page 125, cut out the felt pieces to make the hairband pad. Sew all the pieces together using a running stitch, leaving a small opening to stuff the pad, and then close up the hole with a couple of stitches.

6. Keep in mind that the pad will be covered in daisies so don't worry about perfect neatness. Glue it, using a glue gun, to your hairband.

7. Now begin sticking all the flowers onto the pad, using a glue gun. Start by evenly distributing the largest flowers first so you get an even spread.

8. Then add the medium-sized flowers, and, finally, use the smallest flowers to fill any gaps. Make sure you cover it from all angles, including the sides and the back.

Put it on, and feel like an Egyptian queen!

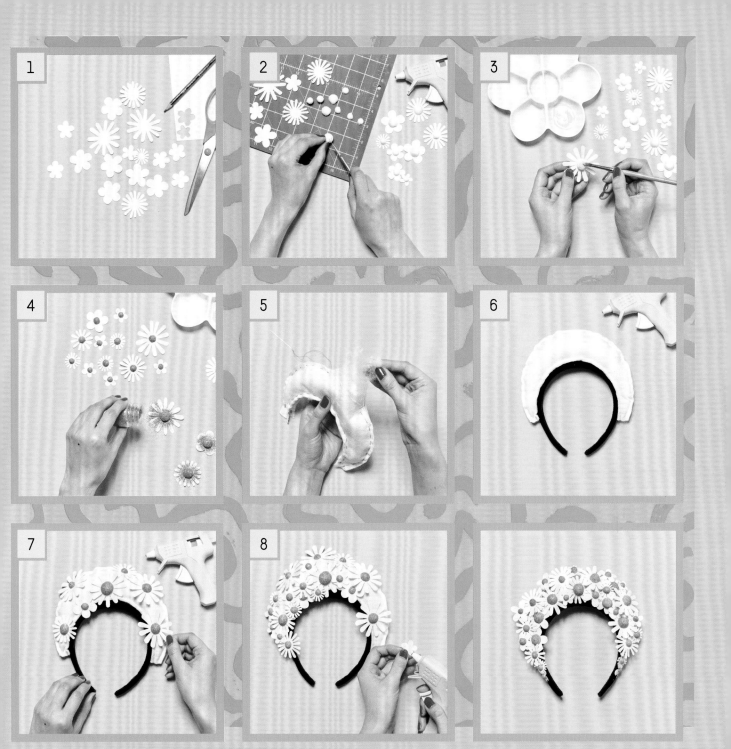

KNIT KNOT BRACELET AND NECKLACE

I was given my first 'knitting nancy' doll by my Granny, when I was a child.

Granny was a knitter and sewer, who gave handmade presents and made excellent miniature clothes for all my toys. I learnt to use the knitting doll with her, and as I've grown up I've collected a few more and have never really stopped using them – probably because they remind me of her.

After many years spent making endless lengths of knitted worms, I decided that I needed to think of a more interesting way to use my French knitting doll.

Things you need: Bracelet

knitting doll (or a pair
   of knitting needles or
   crochet hook)
wool, in any colours of
   your choice
scissors
knot pattern on page 52
2 tassel end
large needle
superglue (optional)
1 trigger ring

Things you need: Necklace

2 different colours of
   wool, in any colours of
   your choice
knitting doll (or a pair
   of knitting needles or
   crochet hook)
scissors
2 tassel end
large needle
superglue (optional)
1 trigger ring

1. Using your knitting doll (otherwise use knitting needles or a crochet hook), knit six lengths of cord, 40cm (15¾in) long.

2. Turn to page 52 for instructions on how to make the Josephine knot.

3. Try the bracelet on your wrist to find the ideal length, allowing for the tassel end. Cut a length of wool and tie a knot where you want to put the tassel end.

4. Thread a needle onto the knot ends and sew through all the ends to bind them. Then wrap thread around all the ends tightly, secure with a final stitch.

5. Trim off any excess length and for extra security add a blob of superglue to the ends.

6. Push the ends into one tassel end and attach further depending on the type of clasps you have. Some may require an additional stitch or come with a small screw.

7. Double check the fit of your bracelet round your wrist and mark where you plan to attach the second clasp. Trim off any excess length.

8. Repeat steps 3-6 for the other side, to attach the second tassel end and add the trigger ring.

You can experiment by using multiple colours or metallic cords. If you can't find tassel ends then try ribbon crimps or cord ends, it's up to you.

Josephine Knot

The world of knots is big and mind-boggling, so don't worry if it takes you a while to figure out. The Knit Knot Bracelet on page 50, is made with what is known as a Sailor's knot or a Josephine knot, but you could use others if you wish.

It would also work with four or two strands, if knitting six is too much for you.

1. Work off a flat surface, or somewhere you can secure the ends of your cord so they don't move around while you are making your knot. You should have six cords in total, two lots of three strands.

2. To make your knot. Take the left cord (three strands), and loop it under itself.

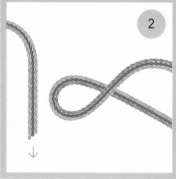

3. Take your right cord (three strands) and place it over the loop of the left cord. Continuing with the right cord, carry it under the end of the left cord.

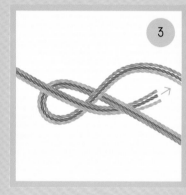

4. Then take the right cord, and carry it over the left cord so that is coming from the knot up top. Move the right loop under the left loop, moving it over itself and under the last bit of left cord. Basically, it is over-under-over-under from left to right.

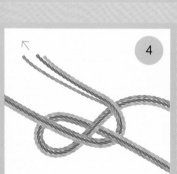

5. Tighten your knot by pulling the ends.

If you knit or crochet, you can use one of those methods to make cords. Or, if you prefer, you can buy cord from a haberdashery.

1. Select a colour of wool, and knit a 160cm [63in] length of cord using a knitting doll. Finger knit the cord, as follows: make a loop at one end of the cord.

2. Using your thumb and forefinger, go through the loop and grab the loose cord.

3. Pull the cord through the loop to make another loop.

4. Pull the loose cord a little to get the loop back down to its original size. It is important here to remember your tension, in order to ensure all the knots remain the same size.

5. Repeat this process, putting your fingers through the loop and pulling the cord through, until you get to the end of the cord.

6. Push the ends into one tassel end and attach further depending on what clasps you have. Some may require a stitch or come with a small screw. Join the tassel ends together with a trigger ring.

7. Using your second chosen colour of wool, make a tassel, following the instructions given on page 12. Tie the tassel onto the trigger ring.

8. Wrap the thread round the ring a few times and tie another knot, before taking the thread down into the tassel to conceal the ends.

CHIC IN ANY COLOURWAY!

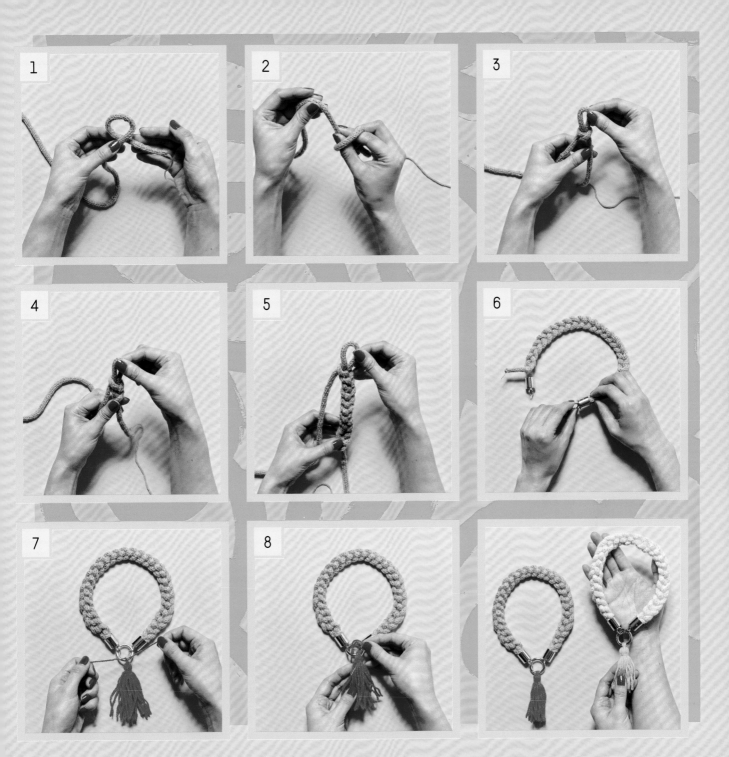

INKY
BADGES

Fully messy and accidental, these come out a bit different every time, in a good way!

Painting on all the colours is the best part, and once you've got a few sheets done, you can make loads with them.

Something about the inks on acetate gives that dreamy stained-glass-window, boiled-sweet sort of look. Make sure you display anything you make against a white background, so you get the full effect of the rainbow colours.

Things you need

acetate
white paper
coloured drawing inks
paintbrush
white mount board or heavy card
spray mount
scalpel
scissors
badge backs
superglue

1. Lay out your acetate on the white paper, this helps you to see the colours as you paint.

2. Paint as many different colours as you like onto the acetate, letting them run into each other a little to create patterns.

3. Continue to add more colours, until you are happy. Leave to dry thoroughly — this can take a few hours, I tend to leave mine overnight.

4. Cut out lots of different shapes from the mount board or card, use the templates on page 122 if you wish.

5. Spray mount the shapes and place them sticky side down onto the inky side of the acetate.

6. Leave these to dry thoroughly and then roughly cut out around the shapes with scissors.

7. Trim down the edges with a scalpel.

8. Attach a badge back to the reverse side of each shape using superglue. Then deal them out to all your friends!

As well as badges these make great gift tags or stick a few to blank greetings card.

FAKE FUR POM

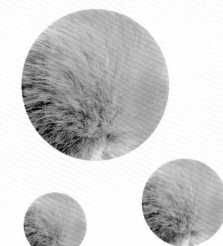

Look at these and tell me you don't want them!

I can't tell you how much joy I get from wearing these furry guys on my feet everyday. If you don't feel brave enough to wear them on your shoes, sew on a jump ring and attach a key-ring finding, or even sew one onto a hair elastic for a cute ponytail bobble.

Whatever you do, just get them in your life!

Things you need

felt pen or a pencil
fake fur material
compass or large roll of
  tape as a template
scissors
needle and strong thread
toy stuffing/wadding
small coin, 2.5cm
  [1in] in diameter
small piece of felt
2 shoe clips
glue gun

1. Draw two circles on your fur material, roughly 12cm [4¾in] in diameter — a full roll of sticky tape is a good size to draw round.

2. Cut out the circles with scissors and put one to one side. Thread your needle with a double length of thread, leaving a thread tail of 10cm [4in]. Tack around the edge of the fur disc, using a running stitch.

3. When you get back to where you started, go back out the disc with the needle so now you have two tail ends next to each other. Hold the disc and pull the tail ends to ruche up the disc into a pouch.

4. Put a small amount of stuffing inside the pouch so it fills out, almost into a ball shape. You can also use your fur off-cuts for stuffing.

5. Pull the tail ends and tie a knot to close up the opening.

6. Thread a needle onto the tail ends and sew a few stitches to secure. Repeat steps 3-6 to make another pompom.

7. Place your small coin on the felt and draw round it to make two circles. Cut them out. Sew a shoe clip onto each felt disc.

8. Attach the back of each felt disc to the base of a pompom, using a glue gun. Hold in place until the glue dries.

Clip the pompoms to your favourite pair of shoes and GET DANCING!

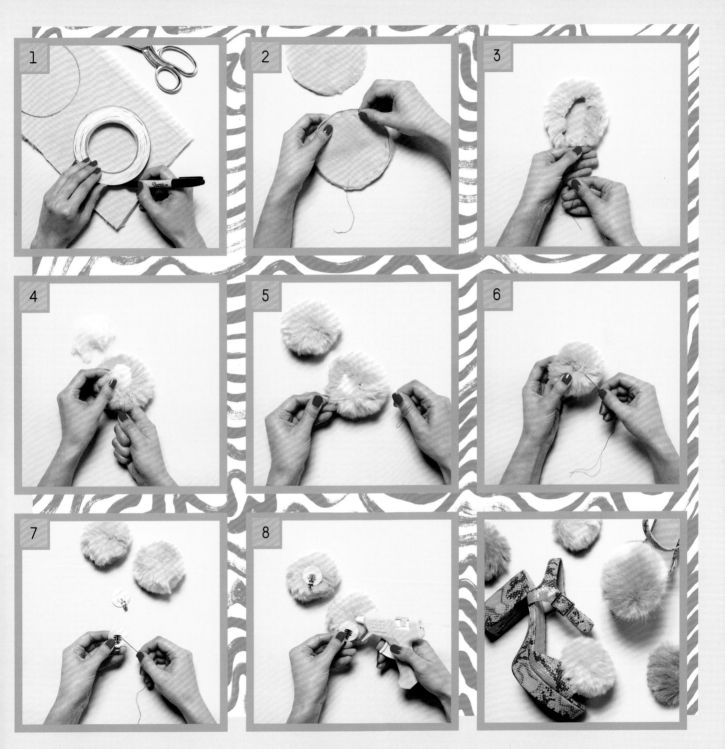

MAGAZINE COLLAGE CROWN

Perfect for anyone who, like me, constantly rips out nice pages from magazines and then never knows what to do with them. I've been saving this cherished photo of Elizabeth Taylor in a folder for years, and finally decided she was the perfect icon for the centre of my collage.

For the base, I've used a plastic princess crown, which you can often find in party or pound shops, but you can apply this method to whatever shape you can find.

Things you need

    magazine cuttings
    scissors
    2 sheets of card
    spray mount or a glue stick
    scalpel
    plastic crown
    pen
    glue gun
    cable ties

1. Browse your favourite magazines and select all the images you like best. Cut them out roughly and back them onto one sheet of card using spray mount or a gluestick.

2. Now cut out each image carefully round the edge with a scalpel or scissors.

3. Roughly draw around the shape of your plastic crown by rolling it along the second piece of card. Give yourself a few millimetres extra around the outer edge of the crown.

4. Cut out the crown shape and the inner sections, using a scalpel or scissors.

5. Lay your magazine cutouts on the card and decide on a composition that best follows the crown's shape. Place the larger images at the back and the smaller ones on top as a second layer, to provide depth.

6. Slide the cutouts off the card and over to one side, taking care to keep them in position. Glue the card to the crown, using a glue gun, for a temporary hold, whilst you thread cable ties through the holes.

7. Continue to add cable ties until you feel like the card is secured to the crown. Trim the cable ties down.

8. Now start sticking your magazine cutouts onto the crown base with a glue gun, large background pieces first followed by the smaller foreground pieces.

STRAW STACK BANGLES

I go through so many rolls of tape, I started to keep the empties while I figured out what I could make with them all. Naturally, when working, I would end up shoving them on my wrist, so it's the obvious place for them to go.

These look best mixed in with other existing bangles, or stacked up in a group, so make yourself a little set.

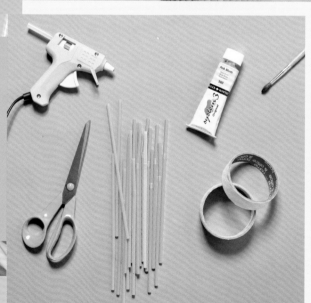

Things you need

empty sticky tape rolls
paint, in any colour to
  complement the straws
paintbrush
coloured drinking straws
scissors
glue gun

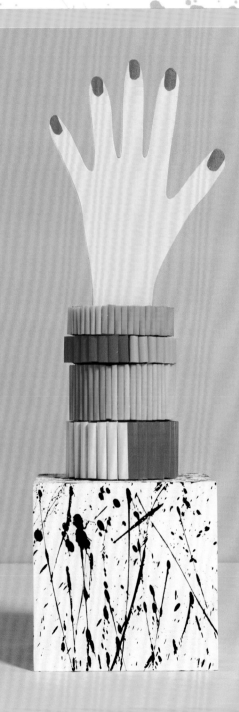

1. Take an old finished roll of tape, and remove any inside labels.

2. Paint both sides and edges with a colour of your choice and leave to dry.

3. Cut the drinking straws the same width as the tape roll. Cut enough straws to get halfway round the roll.

4. Using a glue gun, stick the straws onto the tape roll, by firstly adding the glue onto the roll and then pressing on the straws.

5. Stick the straws on one by one, pressing them close to each other and leaving no gaps.

6. Once you get halfway round, cut more straws in a different colour and continue to stick them to your tape roll.

Make a whole stack of bangles. These always look best in a gang!

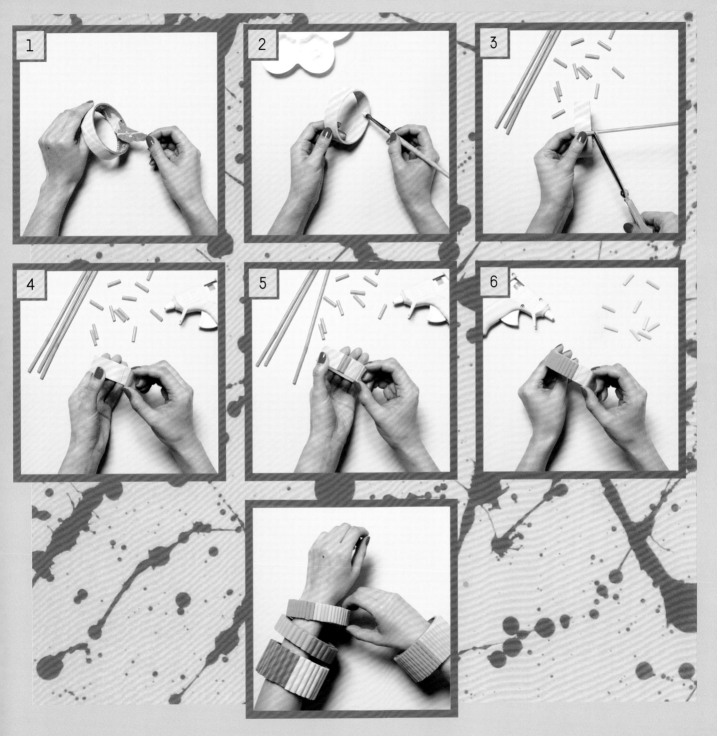

PIPE CLEANER NECKLACE

This will work really well with any coloured pipe cleaner, but these metallic ones provide an extra twinkle that I can't resist!

You can experiment with the size of your loops, or how many you string up. For a shortcut, you can buy some ready-made cord and these necklaces will literally take 10 minutes to make.

Things you need

knitting doll
wool
25 pipe cleaners
piece of card
scissors
needle and clasp (optional)

1. Use a knitting doll and your wool to make a cord 60cm [23⅝in] in length. Alternatively, you can crochet or knit the cord, or use any ready-made cord from a haberdashery.

2. Take a pipe cleaner and wind it tightly round two fingers, to form a ring.

3. Twist the ends of the pipe cleaner round the ring, to secure.

4. Repeat this process with all the pipe cleaners — try to make them all about the same size.

5. String the pipe cleaner rings onto your length of cord.

6. Make a tassel, 6cm [2½in] in length, following the instructions on page 12. Find the centre of your necklace and tie on your tassel, making sure the top of the tassel is level with the bottom of the pipe cleaner rings.

7. Sew on the clasp, or just knot the cord onto it.

SEQUIN BAUBLE EARRING

This technique is often used to make Christmas tree baubles, but, to be honest, I often wish most baubles *were* earrings, so these are right up my street. It's a slow, methodical process, but is really quite relaxing and I'm confident you'll enjoy it once you get going.

For speed, I've used sequins on a thread, but loose sequins are fine too — you'll just need more pins.

Things you need

skewer or bradawl
2 polystyrene balls
  (I used 60mm [2⅜in]
  balls)
1 box of sequin pins
5m [16ft] threaded
  sequins, in any colour
  of your choice
scissors
4 headpins
pliers
handful of bugle beads

6 pieces of coloured foil
  or film, each measuring
  8 x 6cm [20 x 2½in]
small coin, 2.5cm [1in]
  in diameter
small sheet of card
pencil
double-sided tape
glue gun
superglue
2 earring fittings

1. Using a skewer, make a hole all the way through the polystyrene balls.

2. Take one ball and, starting at the top, push a pin through the first sequin on the thread and into the ball, then without covering the hole, wind the sequins around the ball.

3. Secure every third or fourth sequin with a pin, until you get to the bottom of the ball. Secure the last sequin with a pin and cut yourself loose. Repeat with the other ball.

4. Thread a loose sequin onto a headpin and push it through the central hole in one of the balls, adding bugle beads to cover any bare wire.

5. Use pliers to make a hook at the top of the pin. Repeat with the second ball. Use your coloured foil or film to make two pompoms, following the instructions on page 16. Cut the wires from the poms.

6. Draw round a small coin, then cut out. Take two headpins and with pilers bend in half and trim into a U-shape. Stick one headpin to each disc with tape so that the loop hangs down from the disc.

7. Glue the discs using a glue gun, covering the wire and tape. Stick to the back of two of the poms.

8. Connect each wire loop to the hook at the top of each ball, and close up the ends. Using superglue, stick an earring fitting to the card at the back of each pompom, towards the top.

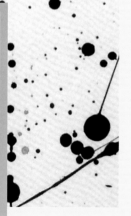

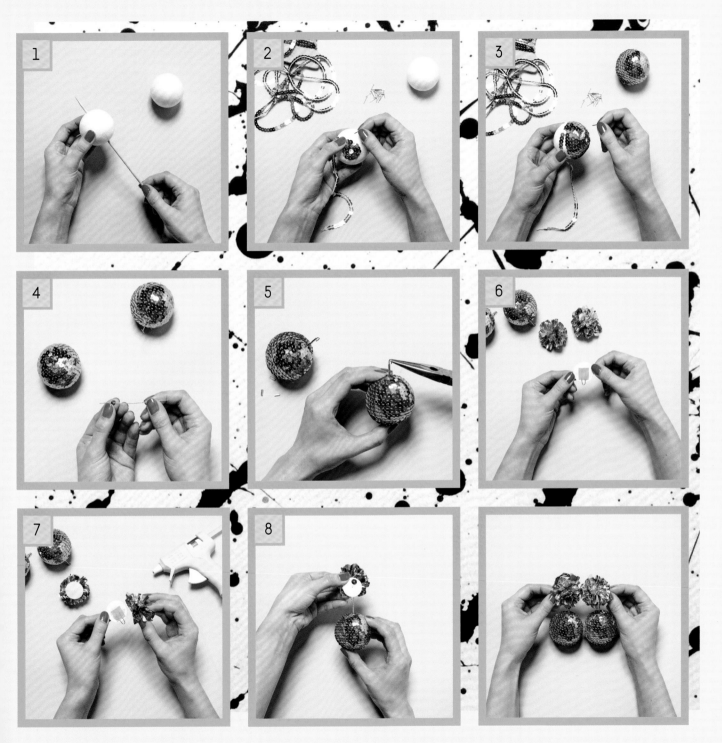

SHOE POM & POM RING

On page 14 you learnt how to make pompoms like a pro. My favourite places to wear them are on my hands and feet, probably because it means I get to look at them all day, but, really, they look great everywhere.

Of course, the colours and sizes you choose are totally up to you. Here, for the shoe pompom, I've used two tones of peach wool at once – this gives a really nice speckled effect.

Things you need

wool
pompom maker
small coin, 2.5cm [1in]
  in diameter
small square of felt
pencil
scissors
shoe clips
needle and thread
glue gun
1 pipe cleaner (for the ring)

1. See page 14 for instructions on how to make a wool pompom. Select a large pompom for a shoe and wind two colours of wool together to get a speckled effect.

2. Place the coin on the felt and draw round it to make two circles, then cut them out.

3. Sew your shoe clips onto the centre of your felt discs.

4. Part the pompom bristles to flatten an area before sticking. Using a glue gun, put a large blob of glue onto the back of the felt and press onto the pompom.

5. Alternatively, leave two long threads on the pompoms and tie them straight onto your shoes.

6. Try making little pompoms and tying them to your ankle strap. CUTE!

1. See page 14 for instructions on how to make a pompom. Choose a small pompom for a ring, and leave two long threads attached.

2. Take a pipe cleaner and bend it round your finger to get the right size for the ring.

3. Remove, then cut the pipe cleaner to the right length, leaving a little extra at each end.

4. Twist the ends of the pipe cleaner to secure.

5. Tuck under your ends so they are concealed, leaving you with a complete circle.

6. Push the join from the ring into the pompom.

7. Tie the threads from the pompom in a knot around the pipe cleaner. Wrap the loose threads around the pipe cleaner a few more times to secure.

8. Tie another knot and trim the ends.

MAKE A WHOLE HANDFUL!

TISSUE PAPER CROWN

Of course, there are a million ways to make paper flowers with tissue paper, so you can always adapt the flower template to your own style. What makes this hairband special is a simple technique using water; it's so effective and gives the tissue that cosmic tie-dye look – so pretty and hippy, I could make this paper forever. Make sure you use a dark coloured tissue paper, so the drops of water really show up.

If you want to play with the colour even more, you can add a few drops of bleach to the water, but just make sure that there is nothing nearby that could get damaged when you flick the water.

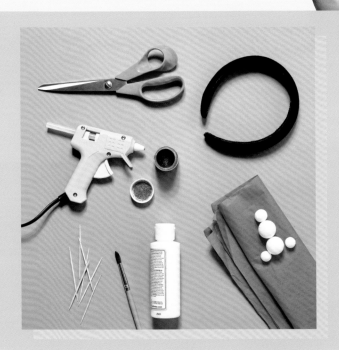

Things you need

3 sheets of dark coloured
  tissue paper
paintbrush and water
scissors
cocktail sticks
approx 8 small polystyrene
  balls (max size 25mm [1in])
paint, in the same colour as
  your glitter
PVA glue
glitter
alice band
glue gun

1. Lay out the tissue paper separately, somewhere you will be able to leave it to dry. Dip your paintbrush in the water and flick the water all over the paper. Leave to dry.

2. Put the dried tissue paper sheets together and fold in half continually, until it's A5 size. Using the templates provided on page 125 as a guide, cut as many petals out as you can, making sure you have a variety of sizes.

3. Take a cocktail stick and push it into one of the polystyrene balls. Mix a pea-sized amount of paint into some PVA glue; this will help to give the glitter a solid base and hide any white areas.

4. Using your paintbrush, apply the glue mixture to the ball, then sprinkle glitter all over the ball until it's evenly covered. Stand the stick in a glass and allow to dry. Repeat for the remaining polystyrene balls.

5. Starting with the smallest petals, add a blob of glue to the cocktail stick stem, just under the ball and stick the petal to it, tightly twisting the paper around the stick.

6. Once you've gone round the ball once with small petals, move up to the next size of petal. There aren't really any rules to this; just add them as you like — it's good if all the flowers look a bit different and vary in size!

7. Lay out your alice band and decide how you want to position the flowers. Put the larger ones at the top and the smaller ones at the sides. Trim down the ends of your cocktail sticks.

8. Starting in the centre with the biggest flower, attach the flowers to the alice band one by one, using a glue gun. Apply pressure to each flower until the glue sets.

9. Work down the sides with the smaller flowers and lastly, place a few flowers so they're facing towards the back. This makes sure the band will look nice from all angles when you wear it.

PAPER LEI

These garlands are so tactile and nice to wear!

In Hawaii, Leis were traditionally given to mark an arrival or departure but they are essentially a symbol of love and celebration.

You can make them for any occasion, but they are especially nice given as a gift. Leis are so easy to make, if a little time consuming, but most good things take a bit of time, and I think these are totally worth it!

Things you need

```
3 different coloured
rolls of crêpe paper
(usually 50 x 250cm
[20 x 58⅜in])
2 bulldog clips
small coin, 2.5cm
  [1in] in diameter
pencil
scissors
needle and thread
wool
```

1. Take one edge of the crêpe paper and fold it over about 4cm [1½in]. Repeat, folding the paper a total of 15 times at the same thickness. Hold the folds in place at each end with bulldog clips.

2. Starting at one end of your folded paper, place a small coin and draw round. Move the coin along the paper and repeat. Continue until you have reached the end of the paper.

3. Cut out all the crêpe discs with scissors.

4. Gently pull each of the discs to stretch them into a soft oval petal shape.

5. Thread your needle and then push the needle through the centre of each petal. Carefully moving the petals along the thread, fluffing them up and checking the spacing is even as you go.

6. Repeat steps 1-5 to make more petals, in the other two remaining crêpe paper colours.

7. Make a tassel following the instructions on page 12. A 8cm [3⅛in] tassel would be the perfect length here.

8. To attach, find the centre of your lei and tie the tassel to the thread, making sure that the top of the tassel hangs in line with the bottom of the petals.

Experiment with size of your petals, the length of your lei and the colours you use.

GOLD FOIL SET

These are made using the paper pompom technique I showed you on page 16. The only difference is that I've used sheets of gold foil instead of tissue paper. Film and foil are a bit trickier to handle, as they don't concertina as well as tissue paper; but it's worth persevering as the results can be really effective.

This gold foil catches the light so well, and I always feel slightly royal when wearing it. If you can't get hold of any foils, then try making this in tissue paper; that looks lovely too.

Things you need

gold foil
wire 10cm [4in]
pliers
scissors
glue gun
alice band (for the headband)
ribbon (for the bracelet)
small piece of thick card and
  ring finding (for the ring)

Gold Foil Headband
1. Cut the foil
rectangles as follows:
Large pom: 8 sheets
14 x 11cm [5½ x 4½in]
Medium poms: 6 sheets
11 x 8cm [4½ x 3⅛in]
Small poms: 6 sheets
8 x 6cm [3⅛ x 2½in]

2. Follow instructions
on page 16, to make a
paper pompom. Using your
foil rectangles, make
one large, four medium
and two small pompoms.
Trim off excess wire
flush with the back of
each pompom.

3. The large pom will be
in the middle, with two
medium poms either side
and a small one on each
end of the band.

4. Put a large blob of
glue onto the centre
of the alice band and
attach the largest
pompom, holding it in
position for 15 seconds,
until the glue has
cooled and set.

5. Continue gluing
all your foil pompoms
onto your alice band,
working outwards from
the centre.

Gold Foil Bracelet
6. Cut out eight
14 x 11cm [5½ x 4½in]
rectangles and follow
the instructions in
step 2. Cut 30cm [11¾in]
of ribbon, then apply a
large blob of glue to
the centre of the ribbon.

7. Hold the pompom on
to your ribbon until
the glue sets. Then tie
it round your wrist, or
attach a ribbon clasp.

Gold Foil Ring
8. Cut out six rectangles
of foil 6 x 8cm
[2½ x 3⅛in]. Follow the
instructions on page 16
to make your pompoms.
Cut out a small disc
of card, 2cm [¾in] in
diameter and stick to the
pompom with the glue gun.

9. Use superglue to
stick the pompom to your
ring finding.

PARTY CROWNS

Simple, but great, party crowns are fun all year round; not just at Christmas.

With a couple of large sheets of card, you can make hats for everyone at your party – they'll look amazing lined up on the table as part of your setting.

Things you need

party crown template on page 124
A1 coloured card
scissors
paint, in the same colour as
  your glitter
PVA glue
paintbrush
glitter, in any colour of your choice
wool, in any colour of your choice
pompom maker
glue gun
double-sided tape or a stapler

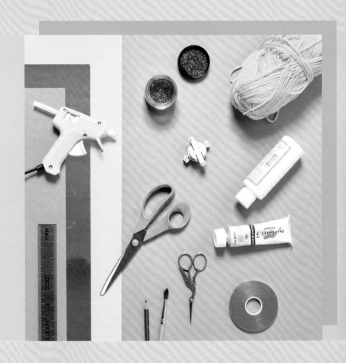

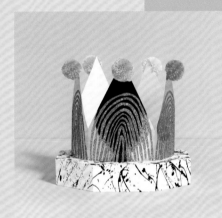

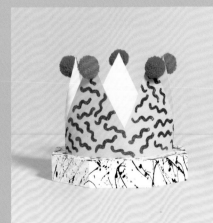

1. Use the template on page 124 to cut your card into a crown shape.

2. Mix a pea-size amount of paint into your glue. This will give the glitter pattern a nice solid base. Using a paintbrush and the glue mixture, create a pattern on the card.

3. Sprinkle glitter over the painted areas while the glue is still wet. It's best to work in sections, so the glue doesn't dry out too much before you apply the glitter.

4. Tilt the card, to loosen any excess glitter, and collect it in a folded sheet of paper. Any excess glitter can be tipped back into the pot to use again.

5. Carry on working in sections along the crown, until you have covered the entire surface in pattern. Leave to dry.

6. Using your wool, to make six pompoms, one for each crown tip. (See page 14 for instructions on how to make a wool pompom). Attach the pompoms to the crown tips using a glue gun.

7. Bend the crown until the two edges meet, overlapping the ends enough to fit your head. Stick them together using double-sided tape, or with a few staples.

Experiment with different patterns and shapes. PARTY!

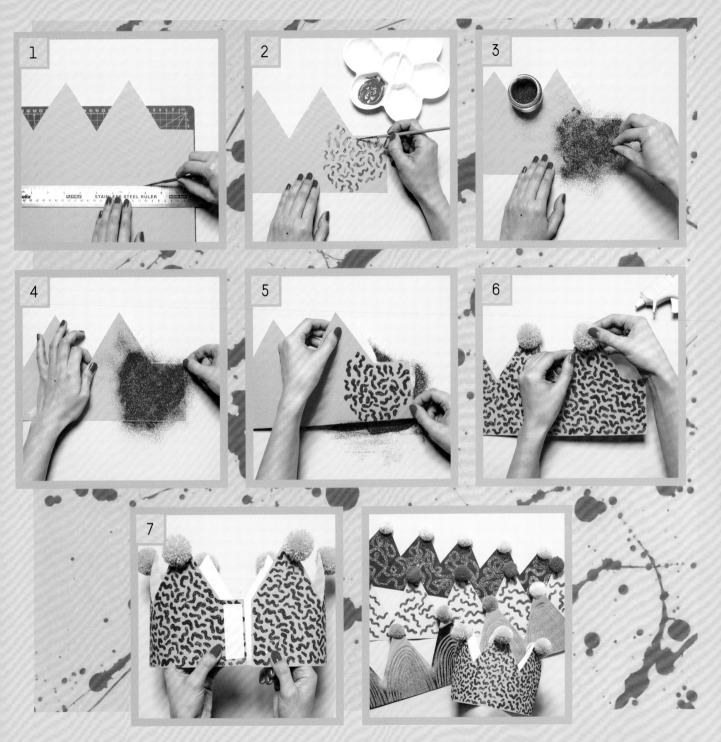

PAINT PATTERN BEADS

Air drying clay was a big part of my childhood. My dad had made an advert for a big brand in the 70s and had loads left over from the shoot. Luckily, it was vacuum packed, because I only began to take full advantage of the huge stash in the back of the cupboard about 15 years later. Any time I was bored, I'd be told to make something with the clay. I made it all – pots, badges, busts, even ashtrays! – but mostly presents for older relatives that I'd dry in the airing cupboard and then cover in paint.

It remains a much-loved material to me, and making these beads feels like being back in art class.

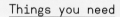

Things you need

air drying clay
skewer or small knitting needle
acrylic paint
medium-sized and small
  paintbrushes
needle and thread
newspaper
clasps (optional)
matt spray varnish

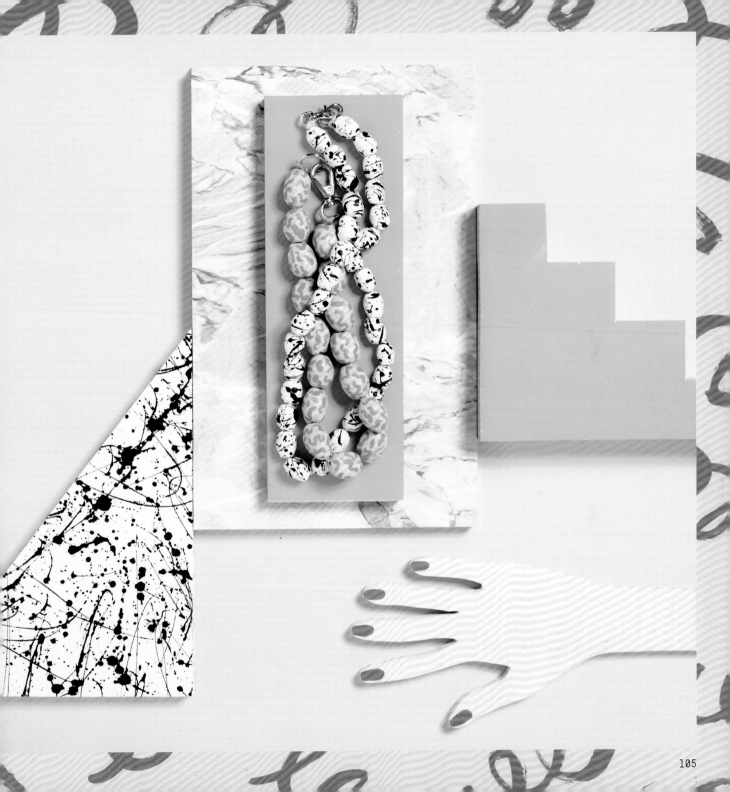

1. Break off small pieces of clay and roll them between your palms, to form small oval shapes — you can make them whatever size you wish.

2. Make as many as required for the length of necklace you want. Using your skewer, make a hole straight through the middle of the first clay bead and, before removing, wet your finger and smooth down the clay a little.

3. Remove the bead from the stick and repeat for all the beads. Place somewhere warm and leave to dry. Before painting, put them back on the skewer. Apply a base of acrylic paint, leave to dry, then add a second coat if needed.

4. Lay down the newspaper and place the beads on the skewer down. Mix a little water into your paint, to thin. Load up your paintbrush and flick it, to splat the beads with paint, all over one side. Leave to dry, then splat the other side.

5. As an alternative try a simple repeat patterns worked in pastel colours, like this.

6. When the beads are fully dry, use a needle to thread your beads. Then try the necklace on to determine the length, tie the ends and trim off any excess.

You can add a clasp if you wish and/or a light coat of matt spray varnish, to make your beads last longer and avoid chipping.

STRAW LADDERS

Straws! Who knew you could make so many things with them?

I have an odd addiction of buying straws whenever I see new ones, in colours I haven't got already. When I was a child, and before the internet, drinking out of a cool neon curly straw at a party was the best thing ever, so maybe I still associate them with having a really cool time as a kid. This set feels a bit native American to me; I guess it's the turquoise colour and the way it's threaded.

As I was making it, I was imagining how great it would look on Pocahontas – what a babe!

Things you need

coloured drinking straws,
  approx 12
scissors
large needle
wool, in a colour that
  complements the straws
clasp
small needle and thread
pompom maker
glue gun

1. Cut your drinking straws into 4cm [1½in] lengths. You will need about 20 cut straws for the bracelet and 40 for the necklace.

2. Thread your wool onto a large needle, then push the needle through each straw, about 5mm [¼in] from one end.

3. Continue to thread all your straws up one side, then repeat this process on the other end of the straws.

4. Try on the necklace or bracelet for size, allowing for the clasp. Add a few more straws to extend the length, if necessary.

5. Using a needle and thread, sew on the clasp. Tie a knot to secure and tuck the ends of the threads down into the adjacent straw.

6. Make a wool pompom, following the instructions on page 14. Tie the pompom around the centre straw with a knot and trim the ends.

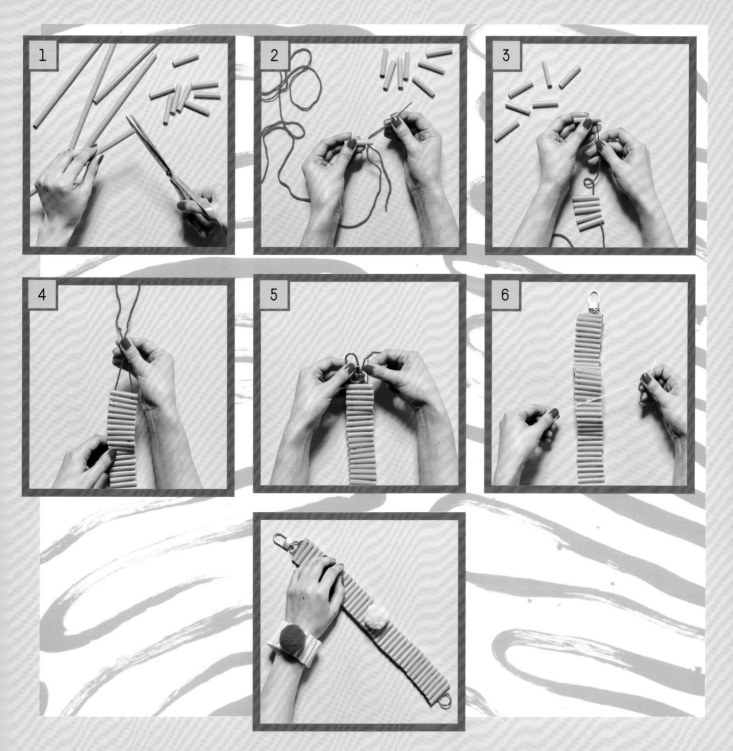

PLASTIC BAG PUFF

**Wearing plastic bags on your head?
Not very glamorous, you may say.**

Well, the bags I've used here come in the most pretty pastel colours and are also scented, and that's good enough for me. Living in England, anything I can make that's 100 per cent rainproof is a bonus, so don't be scared off by this slightly weird idea – it's fun *and* practical. You can use any sort of plastic bags or rubbish bags for this project.

If my final pieces look a bit larger than you'd like, just make the strips smaller for a more modest puff size. Enjoy wearing out in the rain, or for a wonderful bathtime look.

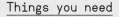

Things you need

plain, coloured roll of plastic bags
scissors
1 metre [3.28ft] of elastic
alice band
elastic hairband
needle and thread

1. To make a headband, lay out three bags on top of each other. Cut off the handles and the bottom of the bag.

2. Cut the bag into strips approx 15 x 8cm [6 x 3⅛in] wide and pile them on top of each other.

3. Pinch the strips in the middle.

4. Secure by tying elastic around the middle, leaving the ends long.

5. Separate each of the layers by rubbing the strips between your fingers and puffing them up. Repeat to make a total of three puffs.

6. Tie them onto your alice band using the elastic ends.

7. For the corsage, make one puff, as shown above. Sew or tie onto an elastic hairband. Wear on your wrist or in your hair.

PASTEL PUFF PERFECTION!

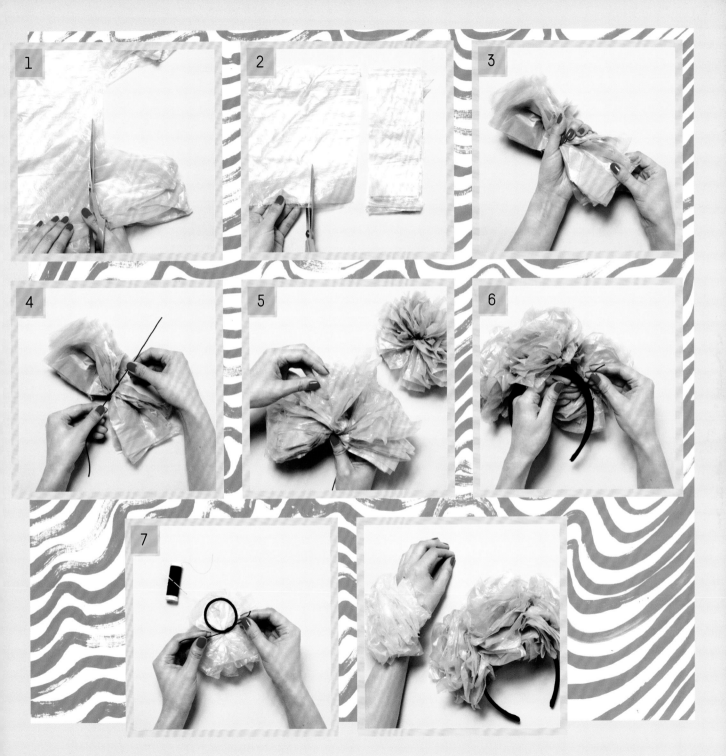

115

MARABOU SHOE AND DAISY GLASSES

This is a perfect opportunity to update any old shoes or sunglasses that you're bored with or don't like anymore.

Pick a pair of glasses with a wide rim, so you have a large surface area to cover. Shoes with a block heel are probably easier to cover than a stiletto, but you can tailor your design to suit the materials you have to work with. Of course, felt flowers and marabou won't last forever if you wear them in a muddy field or on a sticky dance floor, but it will be long enough to get a whole new life out of your tired old accessories. And, it's going to be great fun while it lasts, because these are amazing!

Frankly, this is probably a look best worn poolside, just don't jump in.

Things you need

```
daisy template on page 123
pencil
1 felt square
scissors
PVA glue
small flat-based gems
glue gun
1 pair of shoes
superglue (optional)
1 metre marabou
1 pair of sunglasses (choose
  a pair with a thick rim)
```

1. Using the template on page 123 as a guide, draw daisy shapes on the felt. For the shoes, you need about 25 daisies per heel, but this quantity will vary depending on the size of the heel and how closely you'd like the daisies positioned.

2. Cut out the daisies with scissors, then place a small bead of PVA in the centre of each one and attach a gem. Leave until completely dry.

3. Take one of the shoes. Using a glue gun, add a blob of glue onto the back of each daisy and press onto the heel.

4. If the heels are leather, or any other fabric, you'll probably find that you can stick the daisies using a glue gun; if they have a flat shiny surface, like wood or plastic, you may need to use superglue for this part.

5. Work out how much marabou you need to cover the strap, it may be one or two strips, depending on the width of the strap. Run a line of glue along the strap using a glue gun, and lay the marabou on top. Hold in place until the glue cools.

6. My strap is quite thin so I just used one strip but... if necessary, run another line of glue along the other side of the strap and cover with the marabou. Trim off any excess marabou.

7. For the sunglasses, make as many daisies as you will need, following steps 1-2. Attach the daisies to the rim, using a glue gun. Stick the first daisies on in these anchor positions to get even spacing. As shown.

8. Then start filling in the gaps with more daisies, until the rims are completely covered.

POW! The perfect look for the summer holidays!

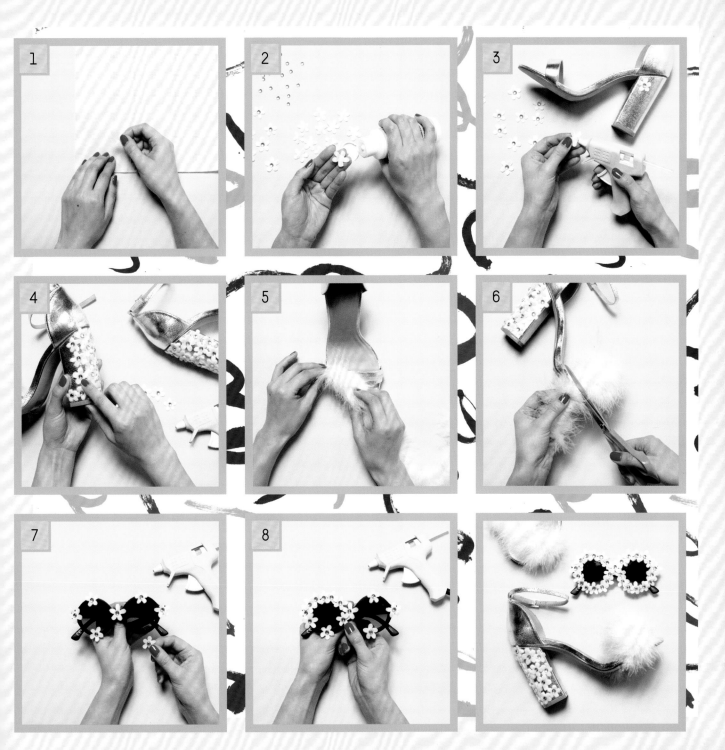

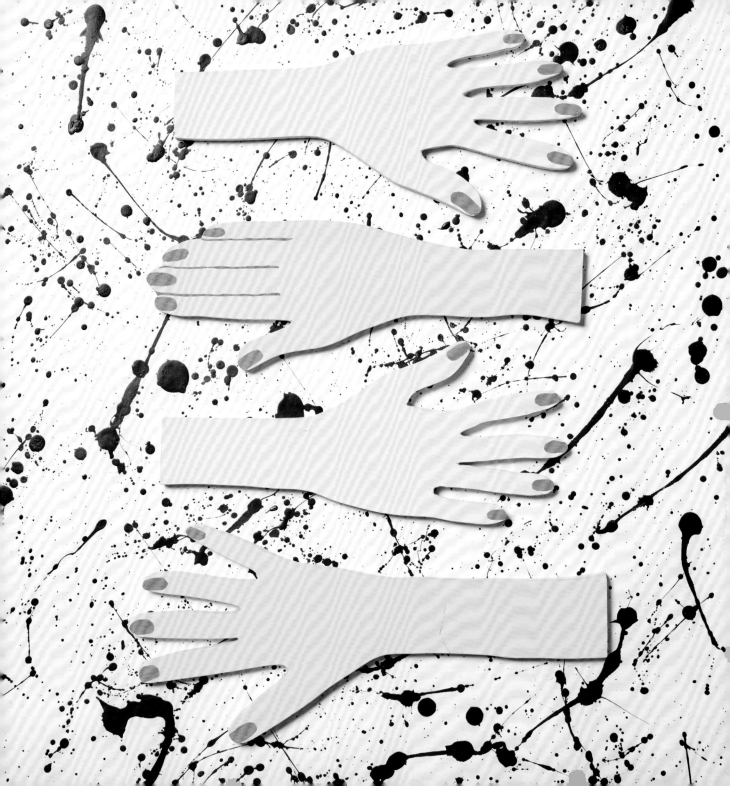

TEMPLATES

Inky Badges page 56
[actual size]

Marabou Shoe and Daisy Glasses
page 116
[actual size]

Daisy Queen page 44
[actual size]

Glitter Ball Earrings
page 40 [actual size]

Daisy Queen page 44
[actual size]

Party Crown page 100
[increase by 260%]

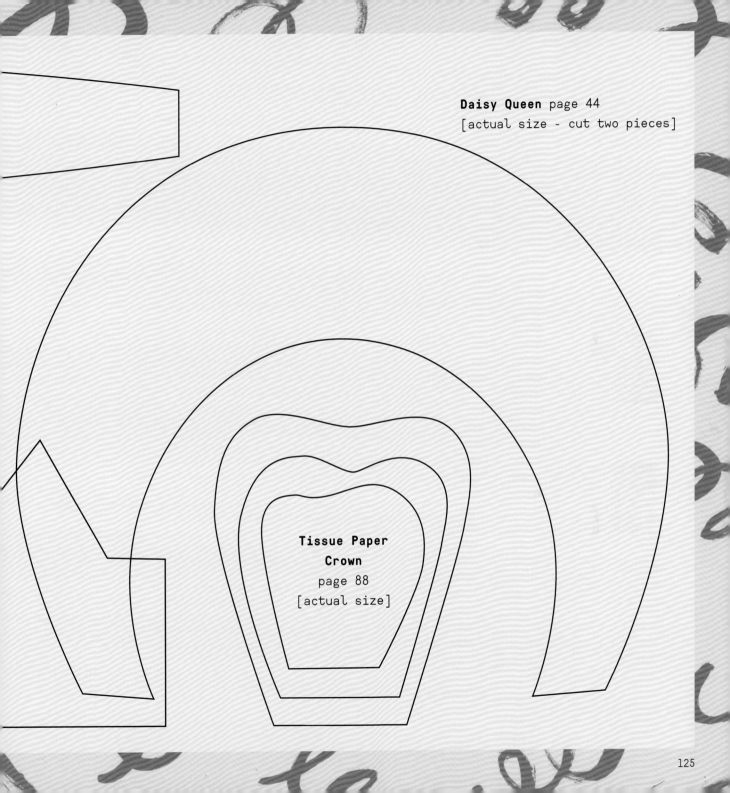

Daisy Queen page 44
[actual size - cut two pieces]

**Tissue Paper
Crown**
page 88
[actual size]

ROSY NICHOLAS

After graduating from Camberwell College of Arts, Rosy began working freelance across a range of fields including illustration, props and accessories.

From her studio in Hackney, East London she draws, paints and glues stuff together for a number of various clients.

Rosy favours simple, yet often time consuming hand made techniques and modest materials to make decorative jewellery and hand painted props.

As a child of art school parents, Tony Hart telly and DIY craft books, Rosy sees herself as a craft based maker, producing opulent objects to decorate both your life and head with!

Past clients include: Selfridges, TOMS, Lazy Oaf, Ace Hotel, Nike, Fred Butler. Kitty Joseph, Estee Lauder, MAC, Andy Hillman Studio, Tim Walker, Adidas, *Grazia*, *Vogue*, *ELLE*, *Dazed*, *Vision*, *Wallpaper*, and *iD* magazine.

SUPPLIES

Materials and Tools provided by Hobbycraft

Wool provided by Stylecraft

Barnett Lawson Trimmings Ltd
16/17 Little Portland Street, London W1W 8NE www.bltrimmings.com

Beadworks Bead Shop
21A Tower Street, Seven Dials, Covent Garden, London WC2H 9NS www.beadworks.co.uk

Cowling and Wilcox
112 Shoreditch High Street, Shoreditch, London E1 6JN www.cowlingandwilcox.com

Dalston Mill Fabrics
69-73 Ridley Road, Dalston, London E8 3NP www.dalstonmillfabrics.co.uk

eBay
www.ebay.co.uk
If you can't find it in the shops, you can find it on eBay. It may not be the cheapest or the fastest to arrive, but there is nothing I haven't been able to find on here.

Ernest Wright & Sons
www.ernestwright.co.uk
Wonderful scissor maker
(see my stork scissors on pages 24, 48, 74, 82, 100 and 108)

Flints – my glitter mecca!
www.flints.co.uk

Hobbycraft
www.hobbycraft.co.uk

John Lewis
300 Oxford Street, London W1C 1DX
www.johnlewis.com

Party Party
9-13 Ridley Road, London E8 2NP
www.ppshop.co.uk

Stylecraft
www.stylecraft-yarns.co.uk

Tiger
www.tigerstores.co.uk

4D model shop Ltd
The Arches, 120 Leman Street, London E1 8EU www.modelshop.co.uk

New Trimmings Ltd
14-18 Great Titchfield Street, London W1W 8BD www.newtrimmings.com

S&K Leathergoods & Fittings Ltd
Unit GB, Leroy House, 436 Essex Road, London N1 3QP www.info@skfittings.co.uk

Publishing Director: Sarah Lavelle
Creative Director: Helen Lewis
Editor: Harriet Butt
Art Direction: Rosy Nicholas
Photographer: Adam Laycock
Designer: Chrissie Abbott
Design Assistants: Gemma Hayden and Katherine Keeble
Prop builders: Tom Hobson and Benny Casey
Production: Steve McCabe, Vincent Smith

First published in 2016 by
Quadrille Publishing
Pentagon House
52-54 Southwark Street
London SE1 1UN
www.quadrille.co.uk

Quadrille is an imprint of Hardie Grant
www.hardiegrant.com.au

Text and project designs © 2016
Rosy Nicholas
Design and illustrations © 2016
Rosy Nicholas
Photography © 2016 Adam Laycock with the exception of page 7 © 2016 Jenny Lewis and 126 © 2016 Nina Manandhar
Layout © 2016 Quadrille Publishing

British Library Cataloguing-in Publication Data: a catalogue record for this book is available from the British Library.

ISBN: 978 184949 787 9

Printed in China

acknowledgements

To everyone at Quadrille, thank you for trusting me with this unexpected opportunity. Thanks to Helen Lewis, Nicola Ellis and Gemma Hayden and especially Harriet Butt, one million emails later, thank you! You've been the best since day one.

Chrissie Abbott, my number one BEB. Having an excuse to talk to you every day has been the real highlight. Thank you for all your work in the middle of the night, you made my book dreams come true from the other side of the world. Love you/miss you!

Tom Hobson and Benny Casey, what a treat to find two set builders as talented and handsome in equal measures. Always a pleasure to work with you boys, another great job done.

Adam Laycock, thank you for making it so fun and easy, it was a dream hanging out with you and the photography looks SO GOOD. I couldn't be happier!

Chinh, thank you for the lending of your lovely hands.

David Westman and everyone at Hobbycraft, thank you for your support and generosity.

Stylecraft, thank you for all the beautiful wool.

Jenny Lewis and Nina Manandhar, I'm so lucky to have such talented women as friends. Thank you both for taking my portrait.

Rose Gardner and Eve Dawoud, thanks for letting me splash in your fountains of knowledge at the start of this project.

Alex Cunningham, everything magically gets better when you're around, thank you for your help and eternal encouragement.

Fred Butler, thank you for convincing me I could make accessories in the first place, I owe you so much.

My sister Molly, my prayers were answered the day you were born. Thank you for letting me dress you up like an absolute freak for the first 10 years of your life. Years later, you're still saving my butt, I would never have finished this without your help. I promise to make you fluffy things for the rest of your life.

My beloved brothers Ben and Dan, thank you for the continuous love and jokes you bring to my life. Villa Armenia forever!

Auntie Rosalie dearest, I'm so lucky to have had you and granny growing up. You had the patience to teach me and inspire me with your ability to make beautiful things. Thank you for all the summer holiday projects and the continuous flow of hand-made presents.

Sammy Davis Jr, what a bloody dream guy. Thank you for loving me and buying me flowers.

And finally to all my friends, Studio 212, Work It family and East London in general, thank you for inspiring me daily and dancing with me nightly. There would be no point in getting dressed up without you all in my life.

rosy